THE
Archive Photographs
SERIES

AROUND UPLYME
AND
LYME REGIS

Uplyme Home Guard at their stand-down parade in the old village hall at the end of World War Two. The Home Guard, formed in 1940 as the LDV (Local Defence Volunteers) in the aftermath of Dunkirk, when the threat of a German invasion was both real and imminent, were due to go to a local firing range on 8 May 1945, but VE Day intervened and they all went off to the old quarry at Raymonds Hill and used up their ammunition in a VE Day Spectacular. Among members seen here are Tom Sloman, Lionel Fisher, Len Copp, Alf Harris, Fred Kingman, Charles Slade, John Currall, Charlie Summers, Billy Stone, Bill Crabbe, Bill Cross, Fred Peach, Mr Fisher, the two Collier brothers, Jim Curtis, Alf Hurst, Hubert Samways, Charlie Slade and John Turner.

THE
Archive Photographs
SERIES

AROUND UPLYME
AND
LYME REGIS

Compiled by
Les Berry and Gerald Gosling

CHALFORD

First published 1995
Copyright © Les Berry and Gerald Gosling, 1995

The Chalford Publishing Company
St Mary's Mill, Chalford,
Stroud, Gloucestershire, GL6 8NX

ISBN 0 7524 0044 4

Typesetting and origination by
The Chalford Publishing Company
Printed in Great Britain by
Redwood Books, Trowbridge

Contents

TOLLGATE. LYME. REGIS.

The Turnpike Cottage at Frost's Corner (named after a Mr Frost who lived there), Charmouth Road, Lyme Regis, c.1910, was demolished around the end of the 1960s. At the time of the picture, the road turned sharp left here and followed the old Roman road to Charmouth. In 1924 the road slipped away; after first following this road up to the golf links, traffic was able to go straight on when the existing main road was opened in 1928. Axminster miller Les Morrish was the last man to drive a vehicle along the old Charmouth Road, doing so on a motorcycle late at night just before the road finally slipped away. Later he said, "I thought it was a rough ride but put it down to having had a few."

Introduction

A cynic once wrote: "All you get from looking back is a stiff neck!" Fortunately few would agree, especially those of us lucky enough to live on West Dorset's beautiful border with East Devon, an area steeped in history and ever conscious of an illustrious past.

It is said that the study of history is a lesson in human nature, the ideal way to understand the whys and wherefores of the development of mankind. Certainly the study of events of the past has influenced much of the planning of the way ahead.

The thirst for knowledge has always been a powerful force. Yet, ironically, the confirmation of what we already know and the recording of what we have enjoyed remain a great pleasure. This is one of the reasons why features highlighting scenes, personalities and events of recent yesteryear are so popular and why this book, compiled by Uplyme freelance journalist Gerald Gosling and Axminster historian Les Berry, is one of many in a series much acclaimed throughout the West Country.

Over 200 pictures, depicting the way of life in Lyme Regis, Uplyme, Rousdon and Combpyne, have been carefully researched and presented with thought provoking anecdotes and captions.

Around Uplyme and Lyme Regis is a pictorial journey from the early part of the century, a truly fascinating period, until the 1950s. Obviously, great change is recorded. Yet, somehow, the very special character of the area seems to have remained constant throughout the march of time. And the tenor of a more leisurely way of life pervades almost every page.

Shots just before and after the last war are numerous, adding to the great appeal of a publication evoking wonderment and magical memories to which many of us can relate.

Throughout, the hand of the storyteller is to the fore, skilfully transporting us to how things were and reminding us of what we are.

David Cozens,
Lyme Regis, 1995

One

Uplyme
a Village and its People

Hook Farm, Uplyme, c.1935. The open space in the foreground is today's car park in Whalley Lane, the lane itself immediately in front of the hedge in the foreground.

Called Fore Street on the two cards on this page, this is the Lyme Road of today as (in the top picture) it passes the New Inn and Mr Saunders's village shop and post office. The post office moved first to the corner of Gore Lane and the main road (see p. 26), then to Venlake Lane, and finally to its present home. These pictures date from around the early 1930s, by which time Mr Irish's butcher's shop, which had been at the end of Stafford Cottages, had been knocked down. Hope Cottages (above right) and Stafford Cottages (below left) were demolished, because it was virtually impossible for two lorries to pass there, and Stafford Mount built in their place.

St Peter & St Paul's church, Uplyme, in around 1905, before alterations. Sadly, the handsome lamps are no longer there. An attractive building with a fourteenth-century tower, St Peter & St Paul's, unlike many of our churches, did not suffer too much at the hands of its 1876 Victorian restorers, although they were responsible for the removal of some handsome Georgian box pews. The six bells were all cast in the seventeenth century.

Mrs Ethelston's School, Uplyme, c.1935. Michael Burge is in the porch. The school was founded by the Revd Charles Wickstead Ethelston, rector at the village for over forty years, and named in memory of his wife who died in 1854. The initials on the weather-vane at St Peter & St Paul's church are his.

This picture of Venlake Lane, Uplyme, in 1890, which shows the debris left by 'a remarkable flood which altered the entire configuration of the land', and the possessions of the occupants of the cottages which had been brought out to dry, became a key exhibit in the re-examination of Harry Stocker in the 'Cartwright vs Axminster RDC' case before Mr Justice Sargant in the High Court of Justice Chancery Division during the summer of 1915. Mr George Cartwright of Bridport Hall in Nottinghamshire owned Hook Farm in Uplyme (farmed by George Bartlett) and sought to restrain the RDC from alleged trespass in a field on the farm known as Venlake Field. Bartlett had put barbed wire across the path at a point where previously there had been a fence and two stiles, the wire being removed by the RDC. Mr Romer KC, for the defendants, sought to prove that a footpath existed in the field introducing witnesses such as Sarah Ann Doble (see p. 29) of nearby Wadley Hill, who testified to having used the path for most of her 80-year life. For the plaintiffs, witnesses (mostly employees it must be said) testified that they had seldom seen people on the alleged path and, when they did, they had warned them off. The picture was introduced to support Harry Stocker's testimony that the fence and stiles, parts of which appear to the right of the picture, did exist. The case received considerable publicity in the local press at the time, and most villagers were happy when the Rural District Council won the day.

Church Hill (now Church Street), Uplyme, c.1904. Note the handsome gaslight on the wall to the right and the equally handsome trees in the right background that went to make way for later development.

CHURCH HILL, UPLYME.

Church Street, Uplyme, c.1935. The 30 m.p.h. speed limit ended at the foot of Church Hill, now one-way and hardly safe at 10 m.p.h.

The old iron bridge that took the Lyme Regis branch line over Whalley Lane in Uplyme the day before it was demolished a few years ago.

Cannington Viaduct, Uplyme, one of the first major constructions in concrete in the south of England and seen here nearing completion in 1902. Lyme Regis waited for fifty years for its railway, the first sod even being cut at one stage but the plan falling through. It finally arrived in 1903, the viaduct causing immediate concern when its considerable weight caused a pier and the west abutment to settle in the sandy soil. A jack arch, built to stop any further sinking, proved successful but flagmen were posted at each end to watch for any movement when trains passed over; they stayed there until the line was taken over by the LSWR.

14

Uplyme, c.1926, taken from above Tappers Knap (far right). The railway bridge has been demolished.

Uplyme from Knowle Hill, c.1907. Barbers Lane can be seen in the middle background; to its right the Whalley Lane council estate has yet to appear.

Uplyme below the Black Dog, c.1922. The road here was far too narrow to allow two cars to pass, and after several narrow misses was widened in the early 1930s.

Toll Gate Cottage, Tappers Knapp, Uplyme, at the turn of the century. Until quite late in the nineteenth century, the main road out of Uplyme (and, of course, Lyme Regis) turned right at the Toll Gate and, via Waterside and Higher Rocombe, climbed up to meet the trunk road above Hunters Lodge. Uplyme's modern main street petered out into a muddy track until the present road through Yawl was cut.

16

Rectory (Lyme) Road, Uplyme, seen here around in 1923, just after the War Memorial was erected, took its old name from the Rectory (now the Devon Hotel) behind the long-since-gone high wall on the right.

The old Black Dog Inn, Uplyme, c.1912. After the left hand side of the building had been badly damaged by fire, the inn was rebuilt; sadly, it closed in 1994. There is more than one variation on the legend of Uplyme's black dog, the favorite being that of a ghostly black dog which rushes along the lane at the back of the inn towards terrified passers-by. Even today it is said that few dogs venture into the lane, and those that do cross over to the other side at a certain spot. .

The East Devon Hunt at the Hunters Lodge Inn at the turn of the century and, below, half a century later. Neither scene would be welcomed by today's motorist, who usually drives far too fast down this stretch of the busy A35 part of the Folkestone–Exeter trunk road. But this was once an extension of the Icknield Way, which carried the Roman road from Dorchester to Exeter. When Hunters Lodge arrived is not known, but it is claimed that it was once an actual hunter's lodge. Said to have been licensed since the sixteenth century, the old inn has more than its share of legends, including a highwayman who, having been refused a drink by the landlord before he was hanged just up the road at Green Lane, comes back as a ghost to ask for the drink every time there is a new landlord.

Cathole Lane, Yawl, Uplyme, c.1932.

Axminster Road, Uplyme, c.1905. With the view of the Talbot Arms blocked by the handsome chestnut trees (centre background) the main interest here is the complete lack of development on the left where today's Cook's Mead and Uplyme Filling Station stand. In the background, behind the cricket field, the houses whose gardens run down to the River Lym have yet to be built.

Wheadon's Family Butcher Shop, Uplyme, 1938. Eddie Wheadon purchased what had previously been Henderson's grocers and newsagents shop on the corner of Gore Lane and the main road in 1936, and ran a popular butchers business there until he retired in 1968. In the top picture, his wife Cordelia and their eldest daughter Phylis are in the doorway. He ran his business in an age when home deliveries were still an everyday occurence, doing so with his Austin van (below) in all winds and weathers – even snow and ice.

The Talbot Arms, Uplyme, before 1936, when Henderson's grocery and newsagents shop on the right became Wheadon's butchers shop (see opposite).

Mrs Saunders' sweet and tobacconist shop on the corner opposite Uplyme's Talbot Arms around 1937. A few years later the shop became the post office. Outside are, left to right: Susan Mence, Winnie Cawley and June Cawley (now Mrs Moulding).

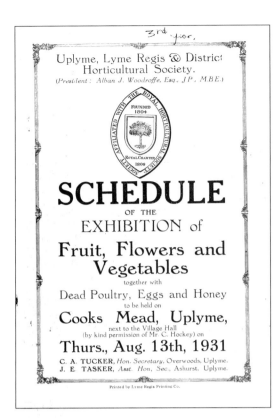

The Schedule for Uplyme, Lyme Regis & District Horticultural Society's 'Exhibition of Fruit, Flowers and Vegetables together with Dead Poultry, Eggs and Honey' for 1931, the Society's third year. It was held in pre-war days in Cooks Mead, Uplyme, rather than on the cricket field as it is now. A glance through the advertments inside brings nostalgic glimpses of the Uplyme of yesteryear, when W.D. Saunders at the post office could supply you with Carters' Tested Seeds and Better Bacon, Mrs Saunders (his wife?), at 'The Shop nearest the Flower Show Grounds' (see p. 21) sold Fruit, Chocolate, Tobaccos and Cigarettes, Harry Hillman at Quaregnon would build you a house (and then insure it for you through Sun Insurance), and Mr Peach would mend your shoes at 'moderate charges' in his Church Street home.

Uplyme Mill (now called the Old Mill), Uplyme, c.1900, when it was also a farm.

Venlake Cross, Uplyme, c.1909.

Lyme Road, Uplyme, c.1920. The small, arched recess in the wall on the right housed one of five outdoor taps that supplied Uplyme with its drinking water. Although some of the taps still remain, this one was removed around the time (1936) Eddie Wheadon began his butcher's business on the right hand corner and knocked down the wall to make room for a shop entrance (see p. 20).

Church Knapp, Uplyme, from Venlake, c.1919.

Uplyme from the Axminster Road, c.1929. The first six council houses in Whalley Lane can be seen in the background.

24

Lyme Road, Uplyme, c.1938. It is interesting to compare this view with that on page 23 and note the changes that took place in such a short spell of time, not least the arrival of electric light poles and the disappearence of many of the trees.

The Talbot Arms, Uplyme, was badly gutted by fire in July 1926, with damage estimated at £4,000. The pub, built around one hundred years earlier, was owned by Mitchell, Toms & Co, the Chard brewers. The fire broke out in the early hours, but the landlord, Fred Tomlin, his wife and son and daughter, and two guests, Miss Pope and Mr Tribble, managed to get out before the place was gutted, leaving only the four blackened outside walls. Axminster Fire Brigade arrived but its only task was to stop the fire spreading to neighbouring cottages, some of which had their contents removed as a precaution. The Exeter Fire Brigade arrived by motor within the hour – which was good going. Lyme Regis's brigade, coming from Dorset, was not allowed to attend.

Uplyme post office just after the turn of the century, when it was situated in the Village Stores (closed only a few months ago). The post office moved to a site opposite the Talbot Arms, then to Venlake Lane, and finally to its present home in the village's main street.

Fred and Kath Cozens in the late 1930s, when the Uplyme post office was on the corner of Gore Lane and the main road, opposite the Talbot Arms.

The dedication of Uplyme's War Memorial around 1921.

Fancy Dress at the Talbot Arms, Uplyme, in the 1930s. The landlord, Tom Sloman, is the clown; his wife is on his right. Extreme right is Mr Burges, while others present include Deverout Mence and Miss Payne.

Workman building the Uplyme Village Hall in 1923, shortly after the laying of the foundation stone shown opposite. The 75 by 30 ft asbestos building took local builder Mr Hillman fourteen weeks to build at a cost of £850. Its first Trustees were A.J. Woodroffe, W. Saunders, H. Jewell, Revd E.B. Bramwell, Miss Jackson and Charlie Hockey. The original managers were Miss Prescott, Mrs Bramwell, Mr Budgell, Mr W. Saunders, Mr H. Jewell, Mr Woodroffee, Mr E.G. Tolman and Mr C. Marchant. According to a newspaper report of the time, the last two were added when a Mr Moss said that 'some members of the working classes' were needed. The following week the paper quoted Moss as saying that Charlie Marchant himself had made the suggestion. A week later Charlie was quoted as saying that he 'most certainly had not'. The hall was opened on 8 November that year with a dance and entertainment organised by the rector. Poppies sold there that day raised £30 11s. A new hall, opened in 1994, was built beside the hall which was demolished in February 1995 after seventy-one years service to the village.

Opposite: John Doble laying the foundation stone of the Uplyme Village Hall on 5 May 1923. His wife Sarah, at 88 the village's oldest inhabitant, had been chosen to perform the ceremony, but she was bedridden and her husband deputized. She was not forgotten – a bottle of sherry was sent her and John kept the silver trowel he used to lay the stone. Happily, the old date stone (1923) has been incorporated into the new hall, which opened in 1994, having been removed and kept until the new hall was ready for it by Bill Crabbe, one of the modern village's 'oldest inhabitants' and a member of the 1st Uplyme Scout Troop which, under ASM Martin, are seen here forming the guard of honour around the stone when it was laid. In the cavity of the stone were placed two documents, a shilling and three farthings.

John Doble, who laid the foundation stone for Uplyme's Village Hall in 1923, lived at Wadley Hill. It was – and still is to older residents – always known as 'Doble's Hill'.

The Start family at Jericho, Woodhouse Fields, Uplyme, 1893. The building to the left centre contained a cyder press.

Uplyme Fete, 1907. The local, but unknown, photographer who produced this card, postmarked 30 July 1907, certainly worked fast to have it on sale within days of the fete. Mrs Etheston's School can be seen in the background, but no Village hall of course. The ladies egg-and-spoon race has hardly attracted the spectators – nor entrants come to that!

The Hoopla stall at an Uplyme fete around 1937, which was run by Mrs Dorothy Mence, centre with the hoops, and her sons, Daddlas, on the extreme right, and Deverout, next to him.

31

Uplyme bell ringers, 1955. Left to right: Revd Seale, Jack Guest, the 'village bobby', Bob Peach, Gilly Peach, Margaret Harriman, Bill Cross, Jack Stamp, Arthur Start, June Cawley, Charlie Stocker, George Tucker, Fred Peach.

The ringers in the tower at St Peter & St Paul's, 1955. Left to right: Margaret Harriman, June Cawley, Bob Peach, Fred Peach, -?-, Gilly Peach.

Mrs Seale, the rector's wife, and George Tucker, sexton, with the seventeenth-century bells at St Peter & St Paul's church after they had been recast in 1959.

Mrs Ethelston's School, Uplyme, c.1924. Back row, left to right: Frank Restorick, Hilda Greening, Fido Crabbe, Nellie Gudge, Dick Finnimore, Edith Hockey, Bill Cross, Bessie Gay, Alf Bastin, Rose Furzey, Mr Sparrey. Middle: Frank Hutchings, Hilda Stamp, Stan Welch, Spick Marchant, Philip Irish, Nellie Tapper, Wilf Norris, Laura Keeley, Leslie Tolman, Winnie Start, Stan Cross, Cora Crichard. Front: May Tucker, Stanley Hillman, Violet Turner, Bill Sansom, Nim Marchant, Harry Copp, Nellie Sansom, Hubert Hellier, Eva Copp, Daddlas Mence.

The Crabbe brothers, Frank (left) and Bill, seen here in 1921 at Happy Valley Cottages, were both members of the 1st Uplyme Boy Scout Troop and its band.

The 1st Uplyme Scout Troop, at Ware House, c.1923. Back row, left to right: Cyril Tolman, Frank Bowditch, Rex Woodroffe, Tom Stocker, Wilf Austin, -?-, Bill Dark. Middle: Arthur Gudge, Bill Bastin, Jack Bowditch, Mr Alban Woodroffe, Jack Dark, Bill Crabbe, -?-, -?-. Front: Frank Crabbe, -?-, Alf Bastin, Fred Restorick, ? Beer, -?-, ? Tolman, -?-, -?-. Alban Woodroofe took considerable interest in the scouting movement, becoming both District Commissioner and a great benefactor, not least because he was always happy to throw his grounds open for camping and scout work.

The Norris children at Woodbine
Cottage, Uplyme, around 1913. Left to
right: Ivy (later Mrs Baker), George,
Wilf and Leslie.

Mr and Mrs Charles Stocker, seen here on their wedding day around 1922, must have been one
of the first, if not the first, couples to go to an Uplyme wedding by motor car. The Model T
Ford, seen here outside their home at Loom Cottage, Cannington, and belonging to Henry
Stapleforth, was the second car in Uplyme.

Action during the Uplyme & Lyme Regis-Somerset game, 17 August 1949.

Uplyme & Lyme Regis Cricket Club vs Somerset County Cricket Club, taken during a benefit game for Somerset and England opening batsman Harold Gimblett, 1950. Back row, left to right: F. Tunney (groundsman), L. Marsh (scorer), E. Ware, G. Housden, E. Hill, M. Tremlett, H. Gimblett, N.F. Borrett, H. Stephenson, P. West, W. Angell, F. Abrahams, A. Rutherford, W.A. Baggallay (umpire). Front: J. James, J. Harris, C. Eldridge, N. Bennett, A. Wellard, A.C.V. Telling (capt), W. Luckes, L. Dodd, A.R. Mason, R. Marsh, A.C. Ford, R. Smith. On ground: R. Bosence (scorer).

Uplyme Men's Club in the Cricket Field around the turn of the century. Members present include James Fisher, Jack Quick, Arthur Start, Bob Greening, Charles Greening and Bob Peach, but possibly the main interest will be in the cricket club's old pavilion in the right background.

Uplyme football club at their Venlake Lane ground, c. 1924. One of the more amusing stories in local football took place on this ground during a Perry Street Intermediate League (Devon & Dorset Section) game between Uplyme and Dalwood. The visitors arrived an hour late and the second half was played in almost pitch darkness. A fed-up home supporter went home and returned with a candle which he lit and, marching on to the field, offered to the referee. He was booked for dissent! Among members seen here are Revd Bramwell, centre back row, and Mr Tolman, on his right.

Bill Crabb (right) and Fred Kingman with the three-horse waggons needed to carry the 40 ft pipes used in the construction of the water works at Pinhay, Uplyme, in the late 1920s.

Mrs Ethelston's School, Uplyme, 1926. Back row, left to right: Miss Newton, Fred Hoare, Victor Selway, -?-, Jim Finnemore, Dick Keeley, Dick Austin, Cecil Quick, Nelson Finnemore, Mr Freeman. Second row: Tommy Crichard, Freddie Seward, -?-, Austen Bishop, Arthur Rendell, Tom Matthews, Frank Stretch, Tom Stamp. Third row: Win Stocker, Mary Sullivan, Hilda Hutchings, Sylvia Matthews, Joan Crabbe, Edie Rowswell, Agnes Harris, -?-, -?-, Hilda Norman. Front: Cecil Fisher, Frank Stocker, Joan Curtis, Wilf Tapper, -?-.

Ware Farm, Uplyme, c.1945. Frank Bowditch and Linda Harris are on the steps, John Crabb (left) and Dick Harris (the farmer) on the cart, and Rosemary Harris is the girl on the right in front.

Mrs Ethelston's School, Uplyme, 1931. Back row, left to right: Dorothy Meyer, Fred Meyer, Stan Marchant, Arthur Hutchings, Joe Crabbe, Stan Gudge, Walter Jelly, Ernie Marchant, -?-. Second row: Fred Quick, Roy Stapleforth, Doris Fisher, Hilda Hutchings, Lucy Hutchings, Joan Crabbe, Edie Beviss, Cecil Fisher, Cecil Quick. Third row: Maurice Tucker, Horace Holman, ? Welch, Mary Holman, Olive Welch, Rosie Welch, Eileen Jelly, Ida Quick, Jack Beviss, Bill Stapleforth. Front: Fred Beviss, Ron Tucker, Cecil Beviss, Charlie Hutchings.

Uplyme tug-of-war team, c.1909, in Hacker's Mead. Among the team are Harry Stocker and Arthur Start.

Tom Crichard and his grandson Tommy at Lower Rocombe, Uplyme, c.1925.

Two
Lyme Regis
The Place

The Parade, Lyme Regis, c.1910.

In the early years of this century, the Lyme Regis bookseller and publisher Dunster collected some excellent earlier nineteenth-century wood-cut views of the town and published them in book form. Although seen through the artists' eyes and incorporating artistic licence, they are of considerable interest, showing such long-since-gone parts of the town's past as the truckway to the Cobb along which goods were taken in horse-drawn trucks after being unloaded from vessels. The similarity between this view, which bears the date 10 October 1855, and that on p. 71 is remarkable. The bottom view shows Marine Parade (then the Walk) in 1862 with the cart road which was built in 1853.

The top view is of Lyme Regis from Charmouth Fields in 1860 and, again allowing for some artistic licence, it shows that the town was still very much centred on the Coombe Street area. To the north there was little or no development beyond the Catholic church, which can be seen on the right. Below, we look at Lyme from Holme (Holm) Bush on the opposite side of the valley. Both originals bear a 5 June 1860 date, which makes the artist a very busy man. Below, one of the two buildings that stand out to the left of St Michael's church must be the old grammar school, which was constructed in 1834, but the safety of the tall one to the rear must have been in question even at that time.

The Rhode Hill Fruit Co, Broad Street, Lyme Regis, c.1904. Much of the produce sold here was grown at their extensive gardens at Rhode Hill in Uplyme, where over a dozen large greenhouses (shown below) produced, among other things, cucumbers, melons, peaches, nectarines, tomatoes and all kinds of flowers. There were also large under-glass vineries which, presumably, produced all the bunches of grapes in the top picture.

The Hotel Alexandra, Pound Street, Lyme Regis, seen here around 1906, enjoyed a considerable reputation. It was originally called Poulett House and Gardens and belonged to the family of that name. During the nineteenth century it belonged at one stage to William Pinney, who was MP for Lyme Regis from 1832, when the town lost one of its two Members, until 1868, when it was disenfranchised as a Parliamentary Borough. Pinney sold the house to the Ingram family, from whom it passed in 1884 to the Revd Edward Peek. After his death in 1888 it was bought for the purposes of an hotel, being 'luxuriously furnished throughout, in excellent taste, and the comfort of the visitors generally catered for...the bathrooms and sanitation are thoroughly up-to-date...' As can be seen from the picture below, the grounds of the hotel (they were five acres in extent) had a frontage on the Marine Parade.

An army supply column in Broad Street in around 1880 has brought everyone out to watch the horses begin the long pull up either to Uplyme and beyond or the Sidmouth Road.

The Assembly Rooms, Lyme Regis, c.1912. The Rooms were originally intended to be a place where the better class of both resident and visitor could meet for cards, dancing and light refreshments. They never proved popular for this purpose, however, and before the end of the nineteenth century, most of the premises were being let to the Gentlemen's Club. The building was demolished in 1928. Bradford & Sons, the Yeovil-based coal merchants on the right, later moved their offices to their depot at Lyme Regis railway station.

Broad Street, Lyme Regis, c.1924, with Watson's Garage on the right where Woolworths stands today.

Broad Street, Lyme Regis, c.1900. Of interest here are the plumes of the Prince of Wales (later Edward VII) above the upper window of the Royal Lion (on the right). He visited the hotel in 1856 when aged fifteen. It was this visit that prompted the old coaching inn to incorporate the word Royal in its title. Today's traffic warden might raise the odd eyebrow (or worse) at the sight of the horse bus badly parked outside.

Bell Cliff, at the lower end of Broad Street in Lyme Regis, seen here just before World War Two, takes its name from the alarm bell that once hung in a small fort there.

Broad Street, Lyme Regis, c.1910, when, despite the complete absence of any motor cars in the street, the Royal Lion was already catering for them, as can be seen by the garage sign to its left. The New Inn, on the right, absorbed into the Lion around 1960, also mentions 'garage & stables' above the arch.

Broad Street, Lyme Regis, decorated for Queen Victoria's Diamond Jubilee in 1897.

The Royal Lion and the Three Cups Hotels, Broad Street, Lyme Regis, c.1923. It is of interest here to note that the Royal Lion has taken (temporary) occupation of the building immediately above it which has served, at varying times, as a school (in the nineteenth century), council offices and offices for the *Lyme Regis News*.

P. Booth, Broad Street, Lyme Regis, seen here around the turn of the century, was a celebrated Ladies' and Gent's Boot and Shoe Manufacturer.

The Royal Lion Hotel, Broad Street, Lyme Regis, certainly before July 1904 when John Groves died after some thirty-odd years as proprietor of the former coaching inn. The Lyme Regis–Axminster horse bus seen here ran twice daily to meet the main Waterloo and Exeter trains at Axminster. The service had been in operation since 1880 but ceased in August 1903 when the arrival of the railway in Lyme Regis rendered it obsolete. Thereafter Groves, who was the town's agent for the L&SW (London & South Western) Railway, used a smaller carriage 'to meet all trains' at the local station. Among drivers employed by Groves were Tom Woodman, Harry and Bill Blake, and Jim Steward.

Bickley's Gentlemen's Complete Outfitters and Artistic (his words, not ours!) Millinery and High-Class Dressmaking establishment in Broad Street in 1908. He also stocked various furnishings, drapery, carpets and linoleums.

Bert Lane, General Outfitter and Tailor at 22 Broad Street, Lyme Regis, obviously believed in blowing his own trumpet in this 1908 edition of 'Mates Illustrated Lyme Regis', which was published under the auspices of the Lyme Regis Town Council. He says "Visitors to this Charming Seaside Resort would do well to patronise this Up-to-date Depot".

Mr S. Harris, at number 65 Broad Street, was a butcher of some repute. The premises remain a butchers shop to this day.

Radford & Radford, Broad Street, Lyme Regis, had been established in the town for some fifty years when this picture was taken in 1906. They were surely the original Jack of all Trades, able to offer General Furnishing, Bedsteads and Bedding of good quality, estimates to compete with any London House, hire purchase on easy terms, everything on hire, Pianofortes (from ten shillings a month on a three-year system of payment), land for sale, houses for sale, estates managed, rents collected, Insurance, Fire Claim Adjustments, tax advice for appeals, accounts prepared for creditors (and collected), funerals (at moderate charges to meet all classes), Monuments, Head Stones, furniture shifted and warehoused in their own pantechnicons (as shown above), and, although they did not mention it, we suspect even the kitchen sink!

The Cups (later Three Cups) Hotel, Broad Street, Lyme Regis, seen here in 1906 when the 'Entire Management was under the Personal supervision of the Proprietress Mrs Garrod', was the town's oldest established hotel, with its own private walk to the Parade. Like its across-the-road neighbour, the Royal Lion (see p. 50), it met all trains, offered its own 'Open and Close Carriages and Posting in all its Branches.' The picture below shows the reception room, although what the bicycle is doing parked against the table is not now known. Sadly, the hotel was closed in 1991 and remains so.

G.J. Rendall, Broad Street, Lyme Regis, c.1907. A grocer, tea & coffee dealer and a Fruit and Provision Merchant who enjoyed a considerable repute in the area, Rendall offered 'free deliveries by own vans throughout the District.' It is of interest to note that he also offered British as well as Foreign Wines at a time when wine-making in this country, virtually non-existent since Henry VIII destroyed the monasteries where much of it was made, was still half-a-century or more away from its post-war resurrection.

W.C. Darby, 8 Broad Street, Lyme Regis, c.1907.

Penny & Co in Lyme Regis's Broad Street, which, having been established in 1775, correctly claims to be 'The Oldest House in the Trade.' Presumably they meant in Lyme Regis.

Broad Street, Lyme Regis, c.1904. Just visible on the edge of the road on the left is a long ladder, which may well have been kept there permanently in case of fires. It is of interest to note that George Rendall's shop blinds, on the right, had a hole cut in them to accommodate his handsome lamp, which can be seen opposite.

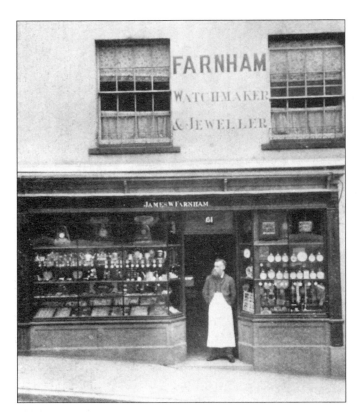

James Farnham standing outside his Broad Street watchmaking and jeweller's business in Broad Street around 1905. Among the many goods on offer inside were Fossil Jewellery in gold and silver.

The Pilot Boat Inn, Lyme Regis, c.1949.

G. Henley's chemist shop in Broad Street, Lyme Regis, around the turn of the century, when he offered for just a shilling a bottle of Health Saline as a 'pleasant and effectual [sic] remedy for Sea-sickness, Biliousness, Headache, Constipation and Derangements of the Liver and Stomach'.

The Fossil Depot, Bridge Street, Lyme Regis, c.1905. Bridge Street was only 7ft 8in wide (a cart width) until the depot and the other buildings on that side of Bridge Street were demolished in 1913 to meet the beginnings of the demands of the motor car age.

The Guildhall, Bridge Street, Lyme Regis, c.1905. More humbly referred to as the Town Hall in some older guide books, the Guildhall was restored in 1887 but it is, arguably, not the town's most attractive building. The Town Arms above the door was the gift of Colonel Pinney, a former MP for the Borough. Local guide book publisher, F. Dunster, at the turn of the century, soon after the restoration had been completed, regretted the loss of an outside staircase which went when the tower was added.

The Philpot Museum, Bridge Street, Lyme Regis, c.1906. The museum, erected at the turn of the century on a site formerly known as Cogmoile Square, was presented to the town by Miss Caroline Philpot in memory of her uncle Mr T.E.D. Philpot (a former mayor) on whose property the museum had been built and from whom she had inherited it after his death.

The mouth of the Buddle (River Lym), Lyme Regis, c.1900. The bridge is said to be fourteenth-century.

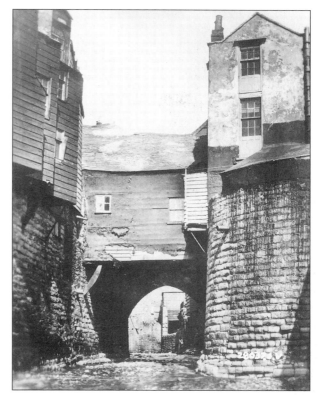

The old stocks at Cobb Gate, Lyme Regis, in the 1880s, with the Pilot Boat Inn just visible in the background. It is not known whether the 'occupant' is just trying the stocks out for size or not!

Pitt House Hotel, Broad Street, Lyme Regis, c.1923. The house takes it name from William Pitt, who stayed at the Great House in 1773 when he was fourteen, ten years before he became Britain's youngest Prime Minister. The Great House was just to the right of this picture; the small wall on the right just inside the iron gates may well have been part of its entrance. It was the home of Robert Jones, a Mayor with a considerable reputation for persecuting Dissenters in the time of Charles II. It is said that Jones had the heads of two of the Monmouth rebels hanged at Lyme placed on the pillars of the gates 'that he might have the satisfaction of beholding them as he walked to and fro'.

Hotel Alexandra, Pound Street, Lyme Regis, c.1910. It is doubtful if any town of a similar size in the country has Lyme's in-depth strength in hotel accomodation. The 'Alex', with its proudly displayed three AA stars to back it up, could justly claim to be the town's flagship.

County Secondary School, Hill Road, Lyme Regis, c.1924. After the school moved to its present home, these buildings became the Woodmead Hall. The site today is the Leisure Centre.

Woodmead Road, Lyme Regis, in the 1920s, when little of its right-hand side had been developed. Notice the complete lack of housing in the fields behind, where today's council estate and subsequent post-war development can be found.

Windsor Terrace, Lyme Regis, c.1906.

Higher Mill, Lyme Regis, c.1890. The mill has long since been converted into flats, while the cottages on the right were demolished to make way for the building of Windsor Terrace (above) around the turn of the century.

Horn Bridge, Lyme Regis, c.1902. The area where the cows are contentedly chewing their cud is today's South, Manor and North Avenues.

Station Road (Silver Street actually), Lyme Regis, c.1904. Morley Cottage (thatched and in the background) is now the Mariners Hotel.

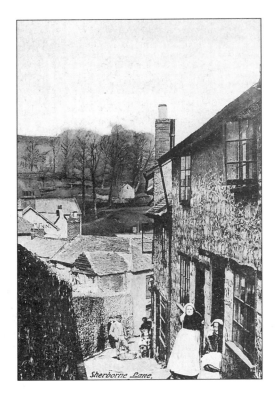

The lower end of Sherborne Lane, Lyme Regis, c.1901. Lyme's association with Sherborne is as old as its history, the first reference to the town being from 774, when Cynewulf, King of Wessex from 757-86 and killed at the battle at Meratum (Merton), gave some land and salt rights at the mouth of the Lym to the Abbey at Sherborne. The lane connects Lyme's old 'town centre' district of Coombe Street with the top of Broad Street.

Sherborne Lane, Lyme Regis, c.1920. The large building in the background was formerly the Crown and Anchor Inn; it closed before World War One.

Although named Pound Road on this 1910 postcard, the view is in fact of Lyme Regis's Pound Street, taken just below its junction with Pound Road. No prizes for guessing from where the street gets its name!

The old Cottage Hospital, Church Street, Lyme Regis, seen here on a 1906 postcard, was founded in 1897 to mark Queen Victoria's Diamond Jubilee. Originally it had three beds on the ground floor for male patients and three on the upper floor for females. Domestic servants were taken if their employers paid 10s. 6d. a week. The building behind, the National (Elementary) School for both boys and girls, was built in 1892, largely due to 'the energy and liberality' of the Mayor, the Revd C. Myers.

The Cobb of Lyme Regis in the reign of Queen Elizabeth

The Cobb, Lyme Regis, seen above in Elizabethan times and below around 1930. The memory most visitors to Lyme Regis carry away with them is of the Cobb. The date of the original structure is unknown, but as early as 1254 the town had ships capable of trading as far as Gascony and it is safe to assume that there was a harbour of some kind at Lyme at that time. The first mention of the Cobb is from 1313, when it was recorded as being either destroyed or severely damaged by storms; later Edward III granted a keyage of a penny in the pound on all goods brought into the town to help defray the cost of its restoration.

The Harbour, Lyme Regis, c.1906.

The Harbour, Lyme Regis, c.1906. The origins of the Cobb are lost in the mists of antiquity, but by the middle of the seventeenth century the old Elizabethan pier of timber baulks had been replaced by a much more solid stone construction which was capable of housing many fair sized vessels, as seen here.

Monmouth Beach and the Cobb, Lyme Regis, c.1896, with part of the cement works in the foreground.

MARINE PARADE LOOKING EAST,
LYME REGIS.

Marine Parade, Lyme Regis, c.1920.

Marine Parade, Lyme Regis, c.1905, looking east. Of interest here is the lack of development around today's Bay Hotel, and the old, grass-topped sea wall.

Marine Parade, Lyme Regis, c.1905, looking west. At this time nothing on wheels that was drawn by any animal could be driven on the Parade, nor was cycling permitted. There was, however, a lower cart track to enable goods to be brought to and from the Cobb, but it did not run the whole way and the beginning (or ending, depending on which way you were going) of the journey was on the sands, or even, as in the top picture, in the sea itself.

Marine Parade, Lyme Regis, c.1930.

The Parade, Lyme Regis, from the Langmoor Gardens, c.1929.

The old Bonded Warehouse, Lyme Regis, c.1930.

The Cobb area of Lyme Regis from the the Cobb Pier, c.1908. Note the lack of development around the Sidmouth Road area in the left background.

The Lynch, Lyme Regis, c.1925. Compare the building on the left with the picture of it on p. 105.

The old coast road from Charmouth to Lyme Regis (Charmouth Cutting). Like most of the cliffs around Lyme Regis, this area had a long history of land slipping, this part of the road falling away in 1924 (see p. 6) after having been in use for some eighteen centuries or more. It was a slip road (no pun intended) from the Roman Durnovaria–Isca (Dorchester–Exeter) road that connected the port at Seaton and the stone at Beer with the rest of the Roman world. It ran north of the then non-existent Lyme Regis, following the Colway Lane–Roman Road–Clappentail line and then on, via the A35, to rejoin its parent just outside Exeter.

Three
Lyme Regis
The People

The National Schools (Boys and Girls), Lyme Regis, with the pupils (and medals for all who had attended school every possible day during that year).

Lyme Regis Boys' School, 1912.

Lyme Regis Girls' School, Group II, 1912.

Mary Anning, Lyme Regis's celebrated geologist, was born in 1799 at the family home in Bridge Street, where her father carried out his trade as a carpenter and searched the cliffs for shells and fossils in his spare time. Mary joined him on his rambles, earning much-needed coppers for the family budget by selling shells and suchlike. After her father's death she unearthed the great fossil, first thought to be of a fish but later realised to be that of an ichthyosaurus, which she sold to Mr Henley, the lord of the manor, for twenty-three pounds. He sold it in turn to a private collection and it was later bought by the British Museum. Mary died in 1847 and is commemorated in a window in St Michael's church.

Miss Mary Anning.
The celebrated Geologist of Lyme Regis.

A Fisherman of Lyme Regis

Lyme Regis has a proud history as a fishing town. This now unknown subject, 'A Fisherman of Lyme Regis', on a 1913 postcard best sums up all the hard-working, cheerful qualities needed in such a difficult and dangerous trade. Like most such men, he made his own pots.

Mr Seward, the boots at the Royal Lion, taking a probably well-deserved rest in the gardens at the back of the hotel in the early 1920s. The beginnings of the Colway Mead council estate can be seen in the background; otherwise that side of the valley is singularly free from development. Among his many duties at the hotel was the garaging of guests' cars.

The Seward sisters, who lived with their parents in Providence Place, Lyme Regis, c.1920. Left to right: Nora, Irene and Lily. Nora married William Curtis and Irene married George Curtis, William's uncle, which meant that Irene became her sister's aunt and, of course, William's uncle became his brother-in-law.

"Votes for Women" meeting at Lyme Regis.

The Suffragette Question dominated British politics as much as anything else in the early years of the present century, before the Representation of the Peoples Act was passed in 1918. Male suffrage arrived for all men over twenty-one, with certain exceptions such as felons and peers; the gentle sex was less generously treated, a woman over thirty only receiving the vote, and then only if she or her husband were qualified on the local government franchise by owning land or premises of an annual value of £5. In 1928, however, universal suffrage became the accepted norm in the country. Lyme Regis had often been the centre of political controversy in the past, so it was not surprising that meetings such as this one, held at Cobb Gate around 1906, were so well attended – by both sexes.

World War One arrived in Lyme Regis when the battleship HMS *Formidable* was torpedoed in Lyme Bay with the loss of over 500 officers and men on New Year's Day 1915. Of the three lifeboats that were launched, one reached Lyme Regis with exhausted survivors and some men already dead. The men were accommodated in houses and inns around the town, fourteen of them at the Pilot Boat, where the bodies of the dead men were laid out in a separate room. One of the bodies was that of Able Bodied Seaman John Cowan, who moved when a mongrel called Lassie wandered into the room and began licking him, and was so spared burial with his less fortunate shipmates in Lyme Regis's cemetery (below). Above, the funeral procession, which started at the Drill Hall, makes its way through a packed Church Street towards the church, where Dr Ridgeway, the Bishop of Salisbury, conducted the service. All the town's flags were lowered to half mast and a muffled peal was rung on the church bells.

The badge presented to the Borough of Lyme Regis by the survivors of HMS *Formidable*.

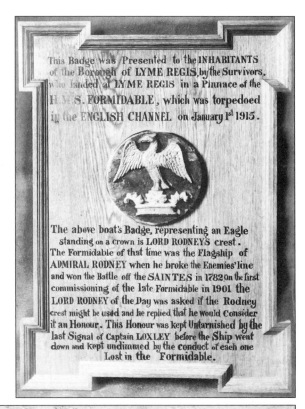

This Badge was Presented to the INHABITANTS of the Borough of LYME REGIS, by the Survivors, who landed at LYME REGIS in a Pinnace of the H.M.S. FORMIDABLE, which was torpedoed in the ENGLISH CHANNEL on January 1st 1915.

The above boat's Badge, representing an Eagle standing on a crown is LORD RODNEY'S crest. The Formidable of that time was the Flagship of ADMIRAL RODNEY when he broke the Enemies' line and won the Battle off the SAINTES in 1782 On the first commissioning of the late Formidable in 1901 the LORD RODNEY of the Day was asked if the Rodney crest might be used and he replied that he would Consider it an Honour. This Honour was kept Untarnished by the last Signal of Captain LOXLEY before the Ship went down and kept undimmed by the conduct of each one Lost in the Formidable.

Mourning cards were brought out in Lyme Regis almost as soon as the *Formidable* disaster was known in the town, the one shown below being sent to Lily Curtis by a Mr F. Beardall on 6 January. When the survivors, who spent twenty-two hours in the water before reaching Lyme, staggered ashore, the Mayor (Mr A.J. Woodroffe) was soon on the scene, bringing blankets in his car which he then used to take some of the men to the Cottage Hospital in Church Street.

In Memory
OF THE
GALLANT SAILORS of
H.M.S. "FORMIDABLE,"
WHICH WAS TORPEDOED IN THE ENGLISH CHANNEL,
On JANUARY 1st, 1915.

They died for King and Country.

"Them also which sleep in Jesus will God bring with Him."

In the 1960s, Jack Vincent, then the landlord at the Pilot Boat Inn, noticed a man reading the plaque on the bar wall which tells the story of Able Seaman Cowan and Lassie. The visitor turned and asked, 'Have you ever met that man?' When he was answered No, he said, 'Yes you have – it is me.' Mr Cowan is seen here with Lyme photographer Roy Emmett and a picture of the *Formidable*. When he and the other survivors left Lyme Regis for Chatham, they marched to the railway station behind the Scout Band with, according to the local press of the time, Lassie running in front. A little-known story of the time tells how local man Mr J. Searle, going into the Pilot Boat, recognised the son of his step brother among the survivors.

Customers pose outside the Dolphin Inn in Mill Green, Lyme Regis, towards the end of the 1950s. Left to right: Percy Lake, Mr Govier, Ben Beviss, Syd Caddy, Mr Cook, Fred Rice, Ted James (landlord). The Dolphin closed around the late 1960s.

The Humphrey twins, Harry (left) and Tony, seen here around 1923, lived with their parents above the old Liberal Club in Lyme Regis's Church Street. Although it was next door to the school, both boasted in later years that, 'although we had two seconds to travel to get there, we were more often late than not.'

Lyme Regis's first charabanc was this Real, an American machine which was brought to the town by Frank Watson (the driver above) around 1922 for his Bluebird Coaches, which he operated out of his garage at the rear of the Three Cups Hotel (see p. 53). There can hardly be a town or village between Exeter and Dorchester that cannot produce a picture of a charabanc outing to Gough's Cave at Cheddar, where a resident photographer obviously did a roaring trade with the tourists.

Frank Stone, bass drummer in the Lyme Regis Borough Silver Band, after winning the West of England Drum Championship at Crewkerne on 26 May 1951.

The 1951 Remembrance Sunday Parade at the foot of Broad Street, headed by the Lyme Regis Borough Silver Band and men from the Royal Air Force Marine Craft Unit.

The Curtis family, seen here around the turn of the century outside their fish shop next to the Guildhall in Bridge Street, also ran the fossil shop at the entrance to Bridge Street (see p. 57).

Fred Aldridge ran his fish business in the old fish market in Bridge Street, Lyme Regis, for some twenty-five years after World War Two. Although he obviously took advantage of local fish, much of his stock came by rail from Hull and Grimsby and, not having a van, he had to push sack trucks up to Lyme Regis station to collect it.

Cecil Quick displays the old wooden post box found behind plaster in the outside wall when the Lyme Regis builders Harris & Quick were renovating Norman House in Combe Street, once Lyme Regis's post office, in 1948.

The Lyme Regis Amateur Operatic Society's 1954 production was *Trial by Jury*. The male members of the cast are pictured here outside the Marine Theatre. Left to right: Charlie Broom, Jack Killick, Derek Crawshaw, Billy Williams, Fred Perry, Raymond Broom, Eric Millard, Peter Sharpe, M. Mahoney, J. Rattenbury, Albert Lane, Frank Bowditch, Edgar Evans, Alec Richards, and an unknown musician with his cello.

A Lyme Regis British Legion outing around 1950, with Bill Gurd, Bob Kennedy (with standard), Cecil Quick, Ted Rowe, Cecil Searle, Ernie Govier and Charlie Mitchell among those on parade.

Harvest Home at the Pilot Boat Inn, Lyme Regis, in the late 1950s. Left to right: Bill Reed, Bob Dunn, Cecil Wiscombe, George Curtis, 'Cut' Curtis, Les Wilkins.

The Royal Air Force opened a Marine Craft Unit at Lyme Regis in 1937 which rendered great service as part of 19 Group (HQ RAF Mountbatten, Plymouth), especially during World War Two, when it saved sixty-five airmen, three of them German. The Unit, which closed in August 1964, is seen here marching down Church Street after the Remembrance Sunday Parade and service in St Michael's church in 1954. Among the airmen on parade are Norman Gregory, Fred Smith, Geordie Thirwell, Syd King, and Bert Kerry, all of whom married local girls and settled in the area.

Lyme Regis firemen (then the NFS) during World War Two. Back row, left to right: W. Rice, W.H. Hallett (Chief Officer), E. Emmett (2nd Officer). Middle: R. Govier, H. Larcombe, K. Wright,W. Gaitch, C. Wiscombe, A. Wheeler, W. Perry, W. Howlett, N. Bosence, J. Reed. Front: -?-, F. Rice, G. Cauley, F. Perry, D. Bowditch, T. Smith, H.F. Searle, -?-, D. Hardy.

Blanche Richards, wife of the well-known Lyme Regis printer, with their son John, on the beach at Lyme Regis around 1938. The beach tents and huts were on the beach in those days and not the walk.

Lyme Regis Infants' School, Church Street, c.1931. Standing, left to right: Ken Halliday, Leslie Jones, Joan Slade, Maurice Blackmore, -?-. Among the seated are: Graham Cardler, Bruce Collier, Kitty Smith, Barbara Rault, Jean Wiscombe, David Rattenbury, Doreen Cozens, Betty Beavis, Christine Street, Cyril Street, Kitty Gear, Leslie Emmett, Dick Hitchcock, Bill Case, Florence Craknell, Doreen Holman and Lionel Jefford.

William Curtis (senior), who was born in 1822, first earned a living as a tailor but soon took up fishing, a trade in which he became pre-eminent in the town. He married Miss Harriett Moore, with whom he had twenty-two children, but only nine survived, namely Thomas, Robert, James, Samuel, George, William (see below), Richard, Joseph and Sarah. They had thirty-three grandchildren and twenty-three great-grandchildren. All eight sons followed him into the fishing industry. He died in 1908, aged 86, at his cottage home at the top of Church Cliffs.

William 'Swap' Curtis, seen here with his wife, Mary Anne Gorge, outside their cottage just off Silver Street in around 1928, is said to have been the first fisherman to acquire the fishing rights off Back Beach. Mary Anne died in 1947, aged 92, having married four times (William Curtis was the fourth) and having the first Lyme Regis lifeboat, the *Mary Anne*, named after her.

Four

At Work ...

Cloverdale Garage, Charmouth Road, Lyme Regis, in the early 1970s. Demolished to make way for development in the late 1980s, with it went Lyme's last petrol pumps.

Workmen employed on the construction of Woodmead Road Bridge in the 1920s include George Sweetland, Alf Chaffey, Ernie Govier, John Leno and Dave Cozens.

Building workers at Pine Crest, Ware Lane, Uplyme, 1934. Left to right: Will Gatch, Will Rice, George Humphrey, Ernie 'Dink' Marchant, Cecil Quick, Charlie Roberts, Harold Hallett, Charles Hitchcock.

The old cement works on Lyme Regis's Monmouth Beach. Seen here in around 1934, before the arrival of the Royal Air Force Marine Craft Unit and in a derelict state, the works had closed in 1914, the tall chimneys being demolished as recently as 1936.

Labour disputes are not modern problems. In 1913 the Lyme Regis Cement Works had a lock-out, the workers staging a protest march through the town. Compare the small placard centre left which says 'Father In Work' and shows a huge loaf of bread on top with the size of the loaf on top of the placard to its left which states 'Father Out Of Work'. With, as the placard says, 375 people (men, women and children) depending on the works for their daily bread, it must have been a blow to the town when the works were closed the following year. Note, in the background, the demolition of the Fossil Shop (see p. 57) in process during the widening of Bridge Street.

Between 1957 and 1959 the Lyme Regis branch of the British Legion were largely responsible for the building of the extension to the Lyme Regis Hospital in Pound Road. Members busy clearing shrubs here are, left to right: Charlie Govier, Cecil Wiscombe, Charlie Clarke, Stan Parker, Tony Humphrey, Jim Stone, David Vivash and Cecil Quick. Mrs Stratton and an unknown girl are more than interested. The lower photograph shows more work being carried out.

Time for a break, especially with Matron wielding a shovel. Left to right: Charlie Govier, Matron, Cecil Wiscombe (behind), Cecil Quick, Charlie Clarke (behind), Lionel Wiscombe, Jim Stone, Tony Humphrey, Reg Broom.

The opening ceremony, left to right: -?-, Mr R.J. Pratt, Dr Barker, Cecil Quick, David Vivash, -?-, Mrs Lumsden, the Matron, -?-, -?-, -?-, -?-.

Lyme Fire Detachment in action when Amherst Farm, Uplyme, was gutted in the early hours of the morning during the early 1970s. The Lyme brigade were forced to pump water for half a mile along narrow lanes, a problem seldom met with by city brigades.

Not all 999 calls for the firemen are for fires. Here the Lyme detachment clear up the debris after gales had blown off a roof in the Lym Close area in the 1970s. The school buildings are in the background.

Lyme fireman at a drill in the 1950s. Left to right: Mr Shapter, Mr Shotton, John Cozens, Michael Emmett, Reg Perry, Roy Emmett, -?-.

The Mayor, Mrs Bonning, with Station Officer Donald Hardy on her right, at the official opening of the new fire station in Hill Road on 4 June 1954.

Lyme Regis fire detachment at Albert Boalch's retirement presentation, c.1962. Left to right: Gordon Broom, Ray Perry, Donald Boalch, Syd Froom, Jack Evans, Norman Bosence, Charles White, the ambulance driver, Albert Boalch, Merv Evans, Mr Jeffries, Don Hardy (station officer), Arthur Toomer, Gerald Cauley, Harold Durrant, Alan Larcombe, Henry Broom, Roy Emmett.

The Royal Air Force Marine Craft Unit's boat house at Lyme Regis, around 1955. Closed in 1964, it became Lyme Regis's Venture Centre.

William Robert Rugg (1822-1906, seen here in around 1895) was a carpenter who lived at the Cobb, Lyme Regis, having been born in the cottage next to the Royal Standard Inn. His son, another William Robert (1850-1904), was harbour master at Lyme Regis and the family still live in the town.

George Curtis, who was employed by Mr Feltham of Haye Farm, on his milk rounds in Church Street, Lyme Regis, in 1920. Regular customers brought their jugs to the door to have them filled from gleaming brass half-pint and pint measures. Health Inspectors might frown at such methods today, but there can be little doubt that George's well-groomed appearence was matched by an equally well-cared-for cart and equipment.

Lyme Regis railway station, not longer after its Opening Day on 24 August 1903. The first train left for Axminster at 9.40 a.m., the official party of Lyme Regis councillors, the Mayors of Lyme Regis and Bridport, and other dignitaries, travelling at 12.25 p.m.

Staff at Lyme Regis station, c.1947. Back row, left to right: S. Bird, R. Huckle, H. Fewins, T. Woodman, J. Bull. Front: P. Eveleigh, J. Venton, W. Rooks (stationmaster), H. Blanchard, T. Edworthy.

Staff at Lyme Regis station, 24 July 1946. Left to right: Tom Woodman, Bill Green (behind), a fireman 'borrowed' from the Seaton branch line, Percy Bird, Harry Fewins. Harry Fewins spent a lifetime in railways, starting with the LSWR in 1899. He came to the Lyme Regis line in 1917 and stayed there until his retirement in 1950. Plans to bring the railway to Lyme Regis were bogged down for some forty years before Baldrey and Yerbergh started work in 1900. The line was ready for its first train in August 1903. Despite running through East Devon countryside at its best for most of its ten-mile length, it was an obvious candidate for Dr Beeching's hit list in 1963, and after goods traffic had been withdrawn in February 1964 the line was closed to all traffic in March 1965. The track was lifted two years later.

The last regular steam engine on the Lyme Regis branch line (above) ran on 2 November 1963, the line being worked mainly by diesel units after that until its closure on 29 November 1965. The old number 488 tank engine which served the line so well and for so long was built on the 4-2-2 system in the 1880s by the Scottish engineers Neilson Company Ltd. It was used on the old East Kent Railway until 1946, when it came to Lyme Regis, where it remained until 1961. It was purchased by the Bluebell Railway in Sussex and restored at a cost of £17,000; it proved to be a great attraction there.

The New Commercial Hotel, Broad Street, Lyme Regis, c.1906, was one of the few holiday resort establishments that was being truthful when they claimed they were 'two minutes from the sea' – without you having to run to make it.

The Gas and Range Company's works, Lyme Regis, c.1907. Lyme Regis had long been lighted by gas, but it saw many improvements around the turn of the century, including the enlargement of the gasworks and the introduction of new apparatus by Willey & Co of Exeter. The new plant was capable of producing 300,000 cubic feet of gas per week. The Gas and Range Company, which carried a large stock of gas fires, cookers and incandescent lights, had its offices in Poole's Court.

A.M. Burge, tea dealer, Family Grocer and Provision Merchant, Broad Street, Lyme Regis, c.1908. Today the premises are occupied by the Victoria Wine Company.

Watsons Garage (Lyme Regis) Ltd, Broad Street, Lyme Regis, c.1958. Frank Watson opened a motor car repair and hire business behind the Three Cups Hotel in Broad Street in 1921. In 1925 he moved to the premises seen below, which had been built by the Lyme builders A.G. Case and Sons on the site of a former greengrocers shop. Sadly, he died, aged only 37, the day before the new garage opened, having sent the staff off for a day's outing. His son Jack ran the business until it closed in 1962. Woolworths store was built there soon afterwards.

LYME REGIS : "The Naples of England."

Freehold Land
For Sale
For Building Purposes.

Magnificent View of the SEA and BAY.

Close to Railway and Sands.	Roads Sewered.
Gas and Electric Mains.	Good Water.

Tithe and Land Tax redeemed.

Apply to: Messrs. A. & F. WISCOMBE, Builders, LYME REGIS;

HOUSES for SALE

A. & F. WISCOMBE

BUILDERS & CONTRACTORS,
COACH BUILDERS,

The Volunteer Arms (now plain Volunteer),
Broad Street, Lyme Regis, c.1906. Although
claiming to be the 'Noted House for Cyclists
and Tourists', the Volunteer still had stabling
at the rear.

BEER & SON, = Hairdressers, Perfumers, Tobacconists,

28 Broad Street, Lyme Regis.

Private Apartments for Ladies. :——

Marcel Waving,
Vibro Massage,
Hair Dyeing, &c.

ELECTRIC HAIR DRYER.

A large selection of High-Class
Cigars, Cigarettes, Tobaccos,
Loewe and other Pipes.

Proprietor of Beer s Noted Eau de Quinine.

ESTABLISHED 1867.

Lyme Regis's leading hairdressers at the time of this advert (1922), Beer & Son had been
established in Broad Street since 1867.

Old buildings in the Lynch, Lyme Regis, in the 1950s, shortly before their demolition and replacement by Harris & Quick's builders workshop and offices (see below). This walk between the old mill leat and the River Lym is said to have been the site of a leper's hospital.

Coombe Street and the Lynch, Lyme Regis, c.1958.

When the roof of The Cabin (now Lyme Travel Centre) in Bridge Street, Lyme Regis, needed replacing in 1946, the local building firm of Harris & Quick had to 'bridge' Bridge Street with their scaffolding to do the job. Note the then Guildhall Cottage Hotel in the background.

Workers on the job shown above included, left to right, Cecil Quick, Len Fowler, Bob Roberts and Bob Gapper.

Revd Edward Peek (seated right) with his wife and son at St Michael's College at Pyne House in Broad Street (later at the old vicarage), c.1888. The college was founded by Peek, who also built Coram Tower on the corner of Pound Road as a residence for its teachers. He lived at Poulett House (later the Alexandra Hotel, see p. 45) and converted the stables there into a private chapel. After his death in 1898, when the rest of the property was bought for the purposes of a hotel, the chapel, now the Peek Memorial Chapel, was presented by Lady Peek to trustees for the benefit of the church people of Lyme Regis, in memory of her husband and her husband's uncle.

The Yawl Mineral Waters Company at Yawl in Uplyme used a distinctive marble-type glass stopper for their well-known lemonade bottles, examples of which are still dug up around the village. The business closed in the early 1930s and an attempt to restart it around 1990 was short-lived.

Workmen employed by Lyme Regis building firm W. (Bill) Hallett & Son at a now unknown site in Lyme Regis in the 1930s. Among the workers are Ron Govier and Bert Welch.

Five

... at Play

Lyme Regis firemen's tableau at a 1950s regatta parade.

Lyme Regis Borough Silver Band march through the Cobb Gate car park during a Lyme Regis Regatta around 1952.

Lyme Regis Borough Silver Band at a Brass Band Concert during Crewkerne's Festival of Britain celebrations in 1951. The band which was reformed in 1946 by Ernie Wiscombe, and disbanded in 1956, in part because National Service calls prevented a steady supply of fresh recruits, finished first. Back row, left to right: Bill Boast, Jack Burlingson, Dave Tom, Norman Enticott, John Case, Jim Sweetland, John Perry, Pat Perry, Reg Wiscombe. Middle: Bob Gapper, George Broom, Bernard Baker, Harry Govier, Bill Street, Ann Reed, Gordon Broom. Front: Tim Loveridge, Ernie Wiscombe (bandmaster), Frank Stone, Cyril Street, 'Snowy' Miles.

The Lyme Regis Amateur Operatic Society was founded in 1920, its first production coming the following year. After a break during World War Two, the Society's first postwar production was Gilbert and Sullivan's *The Yeoman of the Guard* in the Marine Theatre on 22, 23 and 24 April 1948, when the Society's officials included Albert Lane (chairman), H.J. 'Jimmy' Marks (secretary), H.W. Hayter (treasurer) and Alec Richards (publicity). Among leading performers that year were Roland Stratton, Denis Ellis, Ronald Thomas, Maurice Thomas, Frederick Isbell, Nora Lloyd, Anne Tasker and Molly Raison.

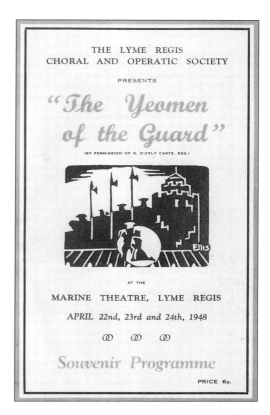

THE LYME REGIS
CHORAL AND OPERATIC SOCIETY

PRESENTS

"The Yeomen of the Guard"

(BY PERMISSION OF R. D'OYLY CARTE, ESQ.)

AT THE

MARINE THEATRE, LYME REGIS

APRIL 22nd, 23rd and 24th, 1948

Souvenir Programme

PRICE 6d.

The Yeoman of the Guard was again the Lyme Regis Amateur Operatic Society's choice for its 1955 production. The cast, seen here on stage at the Marine Theatre, included Albert Lane, Derek Crawshaw, Maurice Thomas, Dorothea Davies, Joyce Whybrow, Ronald Hercock, J. Edgar Evans, William Richards and Donald Gallyon.

The Liberal A team, Lyme Regis Skittle League champions, 1928-29. Back row, left to right: William Curtis, Mr Amos, George Humphrey, Harry Humphrey, Bill Gear. Front: Mr Blackmore, George Curtis, Mr Upjohn, George Hoare, -?-.

Lyme Regis Conservative Club's 'A' snooker side's record in the Seaton Snooker League between 1946-47 and 1960-61 was a model of consistency, the side finishing top six times, second on five occasions, third twice and fourth twice in the fifteen seasons. Members seen here around 1955 are, back row, left to right: Fred Hopper, Charlie Camplin, Dave Rattenbury, Mike Leeming. Front: David Toms, Mr Aldridge, Mr Hammett, Alan Wellman, Ian Cross, Cyril Wellman, Brian Wellman.

Uplyme Skittle League annual dinner and presentation night in the Royal Lion, c.1957. Behind, left to right: Mr Jefford, Danny Watkins, -?-. Sitting: -?-, Mr Powell, George Curtis, Cecil Restorick, George Hoare, Bob Mason.

The Crowning of Mrs Hilda Humphrey (centre) as Lyme Regis Regatta Queen in August 1955 at the Cobb; the attendants are Miss Dinah Bird (left) and Mrs Dorothy Lusk. Also present are Uffa Fox (second right), the well-known international yachtsman and (two to Miss Bird's right) the Mayor, Alderman King. Behind the Mayor is Jack Vincent, licensee of the Pilot Boat Inn for many years; others present include Pam Govier, Stuart Baines, Charles Hallett, Jess Solway and Ted Govier.

Lyme Regis Bowling Club, c.1952, with Mr Rockett, Ken Rowswell, Charlie Broom, Ted Cavanagh, 'Flint' Stone and Mr Challis among those members seen.

Lyme Regis Bowling Club, c.1955. Among members present are Charlie Mercer, English international and national individual champion, and Ken Rowswell, Charlie Broom, Frank Stone, Charlie Mear, Wally Howlett, Peter Law, Tony Halliday, Mr Harvey, Jimmy Curtis, and Cyril James.

For nine years, in the 1940s and the 1950s, the Lyme Regis Branch of the British Legion (the Royal came later) staged a searchlight tattoo at Old Mill. Here, around 1950, the civic party arrives with Mrs Lee Bonning, the Mayor, preceded by 'Goosey' Gollop, the town clerk, and George Norman, mace bearer.

Lyme Regis Fire Brigade, led by Leading Fireman Norman Bosence, at a British Legion tattoo in around 1952. Among the men is Merv Evans.

Uplyme & Lyme Regis Cricket Club 2nd XI, 1949. Members include Tim Bosence, Mike Childs and Bill Matcham.

Uplyme & Lyme Regis Cricket Club, c.1947. Members include Bob Mason, Ray Lewis, Jim Stone and Mr Leas (umpire). At one stage separate clubs existed, both going back to the 1870s, but the present club was formed in the 1930s after the Lyme Regis club had folded and the Uplyme club was in serious financial difficulties. The two clubs amalgamated and have never looked back. In earlier years Uplyme played on grounds at Yawl Hill, Sidmouth Road and Pinhay, before moving to their home at the King George V Playing Field.

Lyme Regis Football Club skipper Bob Dunne being chaired during a procession to welcome home Lyme Bantams Football Club after a cup success in the 1930s. Dunne was landlord of both the Volunteer and the Royal Lion hotels in Broad Street and later played for Seaton.

Lyme Regis Football Club on their old ground on Sidmouth Road, c.1959. Back row, left to right: Brian Walker, -?-, Harry Govier, Brian Wellman, ? Moore, Bernard Gay, Derek Hallett, Robert Broome, Charlie Camplin. Front: Stan Williams, Les Loveridge, Henry Broom, Gordon Loader, Keith Wiscombe.

Lyme Regis Football Club lost 5-2 to local rivals Beaminster in the 1949-50 Dorset Junior Cup Final at Bridport's Crown Ground on 15 April 1950, the first all-West Dorset final. Lyme were 2-0 ahead through Stokes and Wood inside 15 minutes and still led 2-1 at the interval. Beaminster, who were the holders, having beaten Weston United 7-5 the previous season, scored through Cleal, Marsh (2), Newbery and Bailey. The Lyme team, seen here before the game with the Mayor of Lyme Regis, Mr F. King, were, back row, left to right: David Hallett, Cecil Wiscombe, Henry Broom, Clive Enticott, Cecil Hodges (capt), John Perry, Alan Wellman. Front: Tom Perryn, Peter Loveridge, Bill Wood, Wilf Stokes. The bottom picture shows goalmouth action during the game.

Six
Rousdon and Combpyne

Artist's impression of the Rousdon Landslip.

Rousdon School, shortly before its closure in 1939. Back row, left to right: Cecil Murray, Leslie White, Fred Murray, Doreen Webber, Eric Beer, Harold Lanfear, John Rice. Front: Jim Brooks, Eileen Gapper, June Brooks, Sylvia Down, David Slade. The school, built by Sir Henry Peek, who introduced hot midday meals there for a penny (said to be the first such meals in England for village schools), was down to a dozen pupils at the time of its closure.

Rousdon Choral Society, c.1931. Back row, left to right: Mr Crichard, Jack Spiller, Harry Dommett, Joe Body, Stan Carter. Middle: Mrs Summers, Mrs White, -?-, Mrs Spurrell, Mrs Smith, May Matthews. Front: -?-, -?-, Miss Joyce Spurrell, Revd Spurrell, -?-, May Summers, Dorothy Carter.

Landslip Lyme Regis, Dorset.

The Landslip, Rousdon, 25 April 1857. Drawn only eighteen years after the event (on Christmas and Boxing Days, 1839), this picture is of considerable interest, showing as it does the chasm between the 'mainland' and the area, some twenty acres and eight million tons in all, that slipped away before Nature clothed it with trees and bushes. The part that slipped moved around 300 feet, but was intact enough in places for girls dressed as nymphs to reap the already-sown winter corn the following August. There had been a considerable history of instability on the cliffs between Lyme Regis and Seaton, with slips being recorded from the fifteenth century. Although many explanations for the slip were given at the time, the fulfilment of prophecies in the Book of Revelations of St John the Divine being by common consent the most widely accepted, the real reason was one of simple geology. The cliffs were in two parts, with soft, porous greensand and chalk on top of clay and Keuper marl. Water, which drained easily through the top soils, spread out along the top of the clays, and as the joint which acted as a well-greased slide tilted seaward at this point the weight of the top half led to the top layer's simply 'breaking away'.

Partytime at the Peek Village Hall, Rousdon, 1954. Among those about to 'Pass the Parcel' are Mr and Mrs Ben Warren, Cecil Doble, Mr and Mrs Arthur Crichard, Jack Gapper, Hilda Graham, Mr and Mrs Paul, Eileen Gapper, Harry Godfrey, John Godfrey, Susan Bird, Doris Gapper, Mrs Jack Gapper and Mrs Bird.

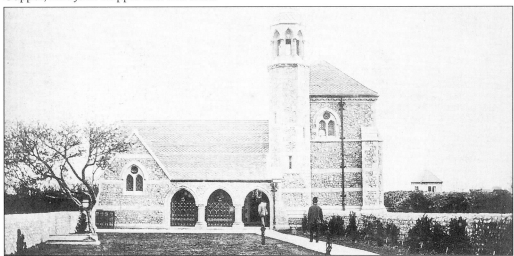

St Pancras's church, Rousdon, seen here not long after its consecration by the Bishop of Exeter on 24 May 1872, was rebuilt by Sir Henry Peek on the site of a much older church that can trace its rectors back to at least 1279, when a Thomas Capis is known to have been there. By the time of Richard Hallett (rector 1814-58) the church was being used as a farm building but the owners, the Bartlett family, are known to have used it for burials until 1840. The new church's nave stood on the site of the old church and had a nave, chancel, chancel aisle and a low tower with a bell turret.

This is almost certainly the funeral of Sir Henry Peek at St Pancras's church in the grounds of Rousdon Mansion, c.1899.

Charton Farm, Rousdon, c.1880, when it belonged to Squire Haymes of Pinhay. Haymes, and Sir Henry Peek of Rounson Mansion, were responsible for improving the road over Trinity Hill to Axminster; prior to that travel was via Uplyme.

Rousdon Manor, seen here in the 1890s, was built by Sir Henry Peek at a cost of £250,000, a huge sum when the work was completed in 1878, but, with an income said to be in the region of a guinea a minute, he probably never even noticed it. The Peek money had been made in the tea trade at the end of the eighteenth and the early nineteenth centuries, the secret of their success being that they could always undercut their rivals – if accounts were promptly settled within the month. The money brought Sir Henry a self-contained town rather than a country mansion; among the many amenities at Rousdon were a carpenters shop, an observatory, a blacksmith, Eton Fives courts, a gasometer, a bowling alley, a laundry, a private church and, by way of oneupmanship of the highest degree over those with mere peacocks, two emus which he had specially imported. Both met sad ends. Sir Henry held many shooting parties, and one guest, seeing just the head of an emu as it walked behind a wall, blazed away at what looked like a particularly plump partridge. The bird died instantly and its mate is said to have pined away.

The North Lodge and Entrance Gates, Allhallows School, Rousdon, 1938. The school was originally in Honiton but its origins are obscure and are thought to have been monastic. By the 1930s, when Allhallows was being run on public school lines under a Board of Feoffees, space had become a problem and the 350-acre estate of Rousdon Mansion was purchased, the school moving lock, stock and barrel when the 1938 spring term was ended a week early for that purpose. Allhallows then became a public school under a scheme framed by the Board of Education within the Endowed Schools Act. At the time there were 160 boarders and 20 day boys, all except the school prefects having to obey a school rule that trouser pockets must be sewn up. Fees in 1938 ranged from £32 a term for juniors (7-10 year olds) to £40 for those over 13 years of age. Necessary extras costing £4 included Laundry, Medical Attendance, Games, Use of Books (which seems rather hard), Class and Laboratory Fees and the School Magazine. Optional extras included Piano, Violin and Organ at three guineas per term, Boxing and Swimming lesson one guinea, OTC ten shillings and Scouting eight shillings.

Combpyne station, c.1954. The only station on the Lyme Regis branch line was reached from the main line at Axminster after steep climbs up gradients of up to 1 in 40. Combyne was axed by Beeching along with the entire branch. The line was finally opened in 1903, after several false starts, at a cost of £67,000.

Combpyne station, c.1939. The station was lit by oil lamps as recently as the 1950s. Of special interest here are the milk churns. They could well be two of the five filled daily with water by staff at Lyme Regis station and sent as early as possible for use at Combpyne station.

Combpyne, c.1923. The central thatched building, now converted into a cottage, was the blacksmith's shop.

Combpyne, c.1910. The 'harbour', as the duck pond is usually affectionately (if rudely) known, was moved to the small, walled plot to its left by Sir Henry Peek when he bought Combyne, reputedly to drive a long-since-gone water wheel. The church of St Mary the Virgin (centre) is one of the smallest in the county. Its saddleback tower, a rarity in England, is almost unique in Devon.

ESTABLISHED 1794.

RETAIL BRANCH
THE WINE SHOP,
SOUTH STREET,
BRIDPORT.

TEL. NO. 2959.

OLD BREWERY,
BRIDPORT.

TEL. NO. 3012.   DORSET

December 19 *5 9*

Mr. J. W. Vincent.
Pilot Boat. Lyme Regis.

Bought of

J. C. & R. H. PALMER

BREWERS.

𝔚ine & 𝔖pirit 𝔐erchants, 𝔐ineral 𝔚ater 𝔐anufacturers.

Our Casks and Bottles are vessels to carry Beer, Spirits and other liquors and are not measures, but every care is taken that they contain their reputed quantities.

| Dec 59 | To 1/4 yrs Rent (Proportion) | £10 | 11 | 9 |

Acknowledgements

We are especially in debt to John Godfrey of the Seaton Book Centre in that town's Fore Street for permission to dig deep into his fine collection of local cards and photographs; to David Cozens for his introduction (David has, of course, faithfully chronicled Lyme's more recent history in the *Lyme Regis News* for some thirty-five years); to Bill Crabbe for his time spent talking to us about the Uplyme of his boyhood; to Axminster Museum for permission to use the picture on page 12; and, last but not least, the staff at the Chalford Publishing Company, especially Simon Thraves, for putting up with us.

Our thanks also go to Derek Baker, Gill Brooks, Winifred Broom, Helen Case, Bill Crabbe, Bill and Mary Croad, Philip Curtis, Cecil Fisher, Violet Flux, Violet Gosling, Richard Gullock, Dick and Marion Hellier, David Humphrey, Keith Jenkin and Uplyme & Lyme Regis Cricket Club, Vera King, Albert Manley, Ivy Mason, Laurence and Jean Masters, Susan Mence, Bob and June Moulding, Cecil Quick, Jack Radford, John Richards, Fred Smith, Jim Sweetland, Joe Turner, Jack Vincent, Ron Vincent and Lyme Regis Bowling Club, Jack Watson, Frank Webber, Brian Wellman, George Westcott and Uplyme, Lyme Regis & District Horticultural Society, Cordelia Wheadon, Dora Wiscombe and Tom Woodman for permission to use their pictures and occasionally send us on our ways refreshed with tea and coffee.